Who Invented This?
Smart People and Their Bright Ideas

Written by Anne Ameri-Siemens
Illustrated by Becky Thorns

This book was conceived, edited, and designed
by Little Gestalten.

Edited by Robert Klanten and
Maria-Elisabeth Niebius

Translated from German by David Henry Wilson

Design and layout by Melanie Ullrich
Layout assistance by Stefan Morgner
Typefaces: Karlo by Sofie Beier, FF Providence
Sans Pro by Guy Jeffrey Nelson

Printed by Grafisches Centrum Cuno GmbH & Co. KG,
Calbe (Saale)
Made in Germany

Published by Little Gestalten, Berlin, 2021
ISBN 978-3-89955-133-4

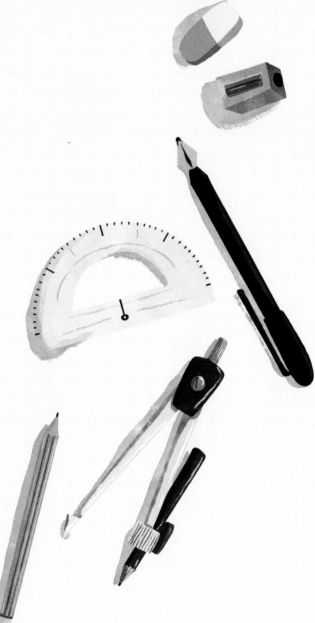

For more information, and to order books,
please visit www.little.gestalten.com.

Bibliographic information published by the Deutsche
Nationalbibliothek. The Deutsche Nationalbibliothek lists
this publication in the Deutsche Nationalbibliografie; detailed
bibliographic data are available online at www.dnb.de.

This book was printed on paper certified according
to the standards of the FSC®.

MIX
Paper from
responsible sources
FSC® C043106

Anne Ameri-Siemens has previously worked for
the German newspapers *Frankfurter Allgemeine
Sonntagszeitung* and *Süddeutsche Zeitung Magazin*,
as well as German television networks. She lives
in Berlin, Germany. *Who Invented This?* is her first
children's book.

Becky Thorns is the illustrator of the acclaimed
Little Gestalten title *The World of Whales*. She
graduated in fine art from Falmouth University,
U.K., in 2015 and now specializes in illustration
for children's books, literary-themed works,
and calligraphic lettering. She lives near the
ocean in Cornwall, in the southwest of England.

Who invented this?

Smart People and Their Bright Ideas

Written by Anne Ameri-Siemens

Illustrated by Becky Thorns

Translated by David Henry Wilson

LITTLE GESTALTEN

DISCOVER THE STORIES BEYOND

Many of the things you have at home were once nothing more than an idea. Look around your room: books, a computer, a smartphone, some Post-its on the desk. Or think of your journey to school. Maybe you ride a bike, or you take the bus, and stop at the traffic lights, and over the weekend you go to the movies or play soccer or meet up with friends for an ice cream. Everywhere you look, you will see inventions that have changed the world. Some are the result of many years spent in a laboratory by individuals or by teams. Other inventions grow out of everyday situations. And some can even be the result of chance. Come with us on a fascinating trip back through history and find out how some people have turned their ideas into great inventions—and how they seized opportunities, had faith in their ideas, and had the courage to try something new.

As you read this book, you will often come across the word "patent." This is a legal protection—when someone invents something, they can register it with the state authorities under a patent, which makes it clear that the invention is their property. With this in place, nobody else is allowed to copy the invention or earn money from it without the inventor's permission.

At the top of each page, you will find dates. They're to let you know when people started to think about the invention. Some of them are quite some time ago!

CONTENTS

BICYCLE

Karl von Drais was the man who set the world rolling.
In 1817, he invented the bicycle. It didn't have pedals
and so was known as a "running machine."

Von Drais's invention was called a "draisine," had two wooden wheels, and could be called "the father of all bicycles." It weighed about 44 pounds (20 kilograms) and had a steering lever above the front wheel.

Its inventor was especially proud of the fact that, on his first long ride of 8.8 miles (14 kilometers) in 1817, he went faster than the stagecoach, which was then the common means of transport. On his bicycle he was able to go 9.3 miles (15 kilometers) per hour.

At the end of the nineteenth century, cycles called "penny-farthings" were constructed with very large front wheels. Mounting these was an adventure in itself. One had to push the cycle until it reached a certain speed and then quickly jump on. Even steering it was a problem.

In 1880, an Italian gymnastics coach, Alexander Giovanni Battista Scuri, built a unicycle very similar to those we have today. However, his invention still had handlebars. Unicycling is a popular hobby nowadays, with competitions and races that include cycling in reverse and slalom.

Many people laughed at the sight of this invention, because it was propelled by the rider's feet running along the ground. The mockers said it looked like someone skating across sand. But it was not long before it had its own fan club. Some historians even maintain that Carl Benz's invention of the automobile in 1886 would not have been possible without the experience and knowledge gained from the draisine. The invention of the bicycle also paved the way for further technical advances, such as the spoked wheel and the pneumatic tire.

Let us now return to the first bicycles. In London, Denis Johnson designed an improved version of von Drais's invention with a steerable front wheel, but still without pedals. This model was called a "velocipede" and was nicknamed "dandy horse"—a horse for posh town dwellers. In Paris, during the 1860s, Pierre Michaux designed the first bicycle with pedals, which were a more efficient way of using the energy from the rider's legs and feet.

In the late 1870s, the safety

Very soon, special clothes were designed to meet the requirements of the female cyclist: divided skirts or wide pants took the place of heavy dresses and corsets.

bicycle, with two wheels of equal size, was one of the most important developments in the bicycle's history: it had pedals that were linked to a chain that drove the rear wheel. This was the beginning of a huge success story. Today, more than 100 million bicycles are produced worldwide every year.

The first cycle race took place in Paris on May 31, 1868. The Tour de France is the most famous cycle race in the world, and is one of the greatest of all sporting events after the Olympic Games and the soccer World Cup. The final stage takes place on the Champs-Élysées in Paris. There are also people who cycle underwater in order to establish records. To do this, there have to be weights on the wheels.

During the 1960s, young people in the U.S. had fun adapting their bikes in order to jump around and do tricks on them. They invented the BMX (bicycle motocross) bike. These can be ridden over bumpy fields and up and down flights of steps, and even in empty swimming pools. Today there are large BMX parks and indoor sports halls, while BMX racing has been part of the Olympics' program since 2008.

Helmets for cyclists were already being produced about 100 years ago. Initially, they were made of leather and had padding on the inside to protect the head in a fall. But it quickly got quite hot inside, so modern helmets allow the air to get in. In many countries it is compulsory for cyclists to wear helmets.

Denmark is regarded as a particularly bike-friendly country. Nine out of ten people there own a bicycle.

TIRES

FROM 1888

You can travel faster on pneumatic (air-filled) rubber tires, and you don't feel the bumps in the road so much. Compared with wood and metal, rubber gives you a better grip on the surface.

Scottish veterinarian John Dunlop certainly never planned to take out a patent on his pneumatic tires. All he wanted to do was help his son Johnny, who kept coming last in tricycle races. We are told that Dunlop himself had never ridden a bicycle before he came up with his invention, but he was interested in rubber as a material.

He had already used it to make different pieces of apparatus for his veterinary practice. These are what gave him an idea: for Johnny's tricycle, he stuck several thin strips of rubber together to form a tube. He wrapped the tube in a piece of canvas and pumped it up, using an old pacifier as a valve. And fancy that! Johnny promptly won his next race.

With his new tires, Johnny won his next race!

John Dunlop

The bicycle mechanic Edlin worked together with Dunlop and tested the tires. They passed the test. Edlin raced through the town on them and was even stopped by the police because he was going so fast!

Robert William Edlin

This aroused John Dunlop's curiosity: could his idea be further developed? He joined forces with a bicycle mechanic named Robert William Edlin. In due course, a professional cyclist used the inflated rubber tires and, after he had won a few races, word spread. Soon there was great demand for Dunlop's tires. However, part of the history of the pneumatic tire includes a man whose original idea was somehow lost. The Scottish inventor Robert William Thomson had already taken out a patent on pneumatic tires 40 years before Dunlop, but this fact had simply been forgotten. Nowadays we take it for granted that we can travel much faster on pneumatic tires—almost all automobile and cycle tires are filled with air.

The first wheels were made from disks of wood, which worked really well. This was about 5,000 years ago. We don't know who invented the wheel or exactly when it happened, but it was lucky for all of us that they thought of it. Otherwise there would be no bicycles, skateboards, or automobiles today.

INTERNAL COMBUSTION ENGINE

FROM 1860

In 1900, there were more than 100,000 horses in New York City. They provided the main form of transport, which meant that about 2.5 million pounds (1,250 tons) of manure landed on the city's streets every day!

There are more than 1,000 million automobiles in the world today. You probably see a lot yourself every day. Have you ever wondered how the automobile was invented?

Nicolaus August Otto was a merchant who traveled a lot. Generally, he went about in a horse-drawn carriage, as was usual in those days. Nobody really knows what caused the merchant to turn his attention to technical matters, but maybe it was because he often traveled for days on end and would have liked to get his business done more quickly. Anyway, he thought long and hard about how one might build a power-driven machine. Perhaps he knew that, in 1860, the Belgian inventor Étienne Lenoir had developed an engine that was driven by gas and air. After Otto worked on his own idea for a few years, he got to know another inventor, Eugen Langen, and in 1864 the two of them founded the world's first internal combustion engine factory. Three years later, they exhibited their "free piston atmospheric gas-powered machine" at the Paris World's Fair. Its special feature was that it needed far less gas than other engines. Otto had further ambitions, though, and he went on to design an internal combustion engine that was driven by a mixture of gasoline and air— the Otto engine. It now exists as a four-stroke engine, for instance, in automobiles and ships, or as a two-stroke engine for motorcycles, mopeds, and lawn mowers.

Étienne Lenoir

In 1863, Lenoir drove his three-wheeled "hippomobile"— powered by the Lenoir engine—5.6 miles (9 kilometers).

In 1885, using the Otto engine as their basis, the engineer Gottlieb Daimler and the engine designer Wilhelm Maybach built the first vehicle powered by an internal combustion engine. They called this two-wheeled vehicle a *Reitwagen* (it was really the world's first motorcycle).

The first *Motorkutsche* (motor coach) on four wheels followed soon after. This was initially steered with a lever.

In two or four "strokes," the Otto engine causes hundreds of tiny explosions per minute. Via different components, the effects of these explosions move the car. This works as follows:

Nicolaus August Otto

1. Intake: The intake valve is opened, the piston moves down, and the space is filled with air and fuel.

2. Compression: The intake valve closes. Now the air can't escape. The piston rises and compresses the mixture of air and fuel.

3. Combustion and movement: A spark ignites the mixture and it burns. The pressure of the expanding gases pushes the piston down again.

4. Exhaust: When the piston reaches its lowest point, the exhaust valve opens. The piston then moves upwards, and the exhaust fumes leave the cylinder. Then the process repeats itself.

DIESEL ENGINE

The German engineer Rudolf Diesel devoted himself to improving the internal combustion engine. He wanted it to use less fuel than earlier engines.

In 1897, Diesel succeeded in getting his engine to deliver 20 horsepower. A new feature was that of self-ignition. This required compression powerful enough to heat the air in the engine to several hundred degrees. When the fuel was injected, it ignited of its own accord. Other engineers had thought this was impossible and regarded Diesel as a dreamer, so he was all the more triumphant when his idea worked. During the years that followed, he was very successful and became a millionaire. He went on developing his diesel engine and looking for ways in which it might be used in other fields. In order to sell licenses to use the engine, he traveled all over the world. But after a few years, his luck ran out. One night, when he was traveling by ship, he fell overboard and could not be saved. How it happened is still a mystery.

Engines are constantly being developed further. You can see this in movies, too: you must have heard of the fictitious British secret agent James Bond. Well, in the films, his equipment has included automobiles that can move incredibly fast, as well as one that could turn into a submarine. After 50 years of driving vehicles with an internal combustion engine, he has switched to an electric one! And more and more drivers are now doing the same.

Rudolf Diesel

The engines that drive airplanes and rockets also work by combustion. They burn liquid or solid fuels. The resultant gas, however, does not move a piston, but shoots out of one side under great pressure and propels the plane forward and the rocket upward.

Thanks to the invention of this engine, people can now build very fast automobiles. But in the animal kingdom, some creatures have a wonderful natural "engine." The fastest land animal is the cheetah, which can reach speeds of up to 70 miles (113 kilometers) per hour. In the sea, the mako shark can swim at up to 35 miles (56 kilometers) per hour.

TRAFFIC LIGHTS

When cars come to a crossroads where it's not certain who has priority, things can get dangerous. That is why we have traffic lights to indicate who must stop and who can go.

Even though traffic lights look different in different countries, the signals of red for stop and green for go are the same everywhere.

The first traffic lights in the world were built in London in 1868. They were worked by hand: a policeman moved the arms of the signal up, and traffic had to stop while pedestrians crossed the road in safety. At night the arms were lit up in red or green.

The idea of using a system with electric signals occurred to several inventors, including the American policeman William Potts. But he also reckoned that, in addition to red and green signals for stop and go, there should be a yellow one for the stage in between.

The yellow light signals the transition from stop to go.

William Potts

Garrett Morgan

In the 1920s, the African-American inventor Garrett Morgan built an automatic traffic light. It was shaped like a "T," and had the signals for stop and go. Morgan sold the patent for his traffic lights to Canada and Great Britain, and became a successful businessman. (He also invented a gas mask and a hair-straightening cream.) More and more traffic lights were erected, with the result that fewer and fewer policemen were forced to risk injury or death through regulating the traffic. Standing in the middle of a crossroads was a dangerous job and many policemen were delighted not to have to do it.

How do traffic lights work today? A signal time plan may determine how long the lights will stay red or green, or these phases can be governed by the amount of traffic. Lights that depend on the traffic are controlled by induction loops. These are wires below the surface of the road that carry an electric current. They create a magnetic field in front of the traffic lights that recognizes that vehicles are waiting.

Traffic lights can also be directed by infrared detectors. These look like little cameras, and they register movements all around them. They, too, can detect waiting vehicles, and green and red periods can be prolonged or shortened according to how many vehicles are on the road. This keeps the traffic flowing, and automobiles and pedestrians never have to wait too long. In large cities there is also a traffic-control center that watches over dangerous crossings through video cameras. The officials can simply press a button if a green phase needs to be prolonged.

In 1933, the first lights for pedestrians were installed in Copenhagen. Nowadays there are even lights for cyclists.

The traffic-light green is not the same everywhere—in Japan the colors are red, yellow, and a bluish green.

In some countries, there are some crossroad lights that have special radio equipment. These can receive signals from emergency vehicles. The apparatus in the vehicle sends the appropriate signal to the lights, which automatically switch to a special program so that only the direction from which the vehicle is coming will show green. When it has gone through, the special program turns itself off.

In the town of Akureyri in the north of Iceland, for several years now there have been stop signals in the form of red hearts. This was the idea of the mayor at a time when many people were worried about their jobs and their future. He wanted to cheer them up.

The figures used in pedestrian lights are not the same in all countries. There are women only, couples, and various characters, such as a little man with an umbrella.

CAMERA

Today it's easy to take photos with digital cameras and smartphones. One click and you have the picture.
We owe this pleasure to the ideas of many different inventors.

The first photos had an exposure time of eight hours! Imagine having to hold still that long so that the picture wouldn't be blurred.

The word "photograph" comes from Greek and means "drawing with light." It's not possible to name an individual inventor of the camera and photography, because over the centuries many people have contributed with their ideas and experiments.

An important milestone was the camera obscura, which means "dark chamber." A camera obscura is a light-proof box (which is also called a "pinhole camera.") Light falls through a hole onto the opposite side of the interior, on which you will be

Joseph Nicéphore Niépce

The earliest surviving photo in the world shows the view from a room. It was taken during the nineteenth century by the French inventor Nicéphore Niépce. He called the process "heliography."

able to see an upside-down picture of whatever is in front of the hole. This technique was described by the Greek philosopher and scientist Aristotle some 2,400 years ago.

In the seventeenth century, a portable box with lenses came into use, which can be regarded as the great-great-great-grandmother of analogue cameras. With these, which many photographers still prefer to use today, you need to have a roll of film.

Aristotle

Louis Daguerre

The next important step for a clear image was taken by the French painter and inventor Louis Daguerre, who designed a process by which pictures could be captured on a thin metal plate.

William Henry Fox Talbot

An important step in the evolution of photography was the invention of the negative by the British inventor William Henry Fox Talbot. His process allowed many copies to be made from a single negative. You have probably seen one yourself: it's a small picture in which light and dark are reversed.

The American inventor George Eastman had plenty of ideas for how to make photography simpler. He developed photographic plates that did not have to be painstakingly prepared in darkness beforehand. You could simply take these new plates with you. Then he invented the roll of film. This replaced glass plates, which were very heavy and initially had to be rushed to a light-proof tent so that they could be developed immediately. With the roll, it was possible to take 100 photos instead of one per plate. Shortly afterwards, Eastman designed a portable camera. By comparison, the cameras that required plates were roughly the size of a microwave.

George Eastman

David Paul Gregg

In 1963, while working at Stanford University in California, the American engineer David Paul Gregg invented the first camera that could store photos electronically. Initially, the pictures could only be stored for a few minutes, but all the same, this Videodisk camera, as it was known, was another major step in the development of photography.

In 1969, the Canadian physicist Willard Boyle and his American colleague George Elwood Smith developed a chip called CCD that could store pictures digitally. Four years later, the first digital camera went on the market. It weighed almost 9 pounds (4 kilograms) and could take pictures with a resolution of 100×100 pixels. Today, a digital camera can achieve more than 20 million pixels.

Gregg's camera could store pictures for a few minutes on a transparent disc.

CINEMATOGRAPHY

When motion pictures began to be shown in movie theaters more than a hundred years ago, the audience jumped out of their seats—not with enthusiasm but out of fear!

Auguste and Louis Lumière

The story goes that during one of the early movie screenings in Paris, people panicked because they saw a train heading toward them. Everyone was terrified that it would come straight out into the auditorium. Motion pictures on a screen were a new and overwhelming experience. The movie was shown through a cinematograph, which was both a film camera and projector, combining lens and light to project the pictures onto the screen. It was designed by the brothers Auguste and Louis Lumière, who patented it on February 13, 1895. With this, they invented the movie theater and created the opportunity to show movies to large audiences. At the time, many other inventors were also fascinated by the idea that photography could be further developed through motion pictures. The German brothers Max and Emil Skladanowsky called their own projector a Bioscop. One of their earliest movies was *Boxing Kangaroo*. Have a look for it on the internet—it might make you jump off the couch!

Max and Emil Skladanowsky

Wow, the kangaroo not only boxes but can also do a great headlock!

23

Leland Stanford

Eadweard Muybridge

Stanford was right: while galloping, horses do take all four hooves off the ground.

And this is how the first motion pictures were made: the horse breeder Leland Stanford (who was also the founder of Stanford University) wanted to find out if, when horses galloped, they ever took all four hooves off the ground at the same time—way back in 1872. In 1878, he commissioned the photographer Eadweard Muybridge to conduct an experiment. Muybridge set up 12 cameras that were triggered by wires that were stretched out on the ground. Through this, he created a sequence of pictures that, when put together, showed the movement of the horse. This was the beginning of something. As Muybridge did not have a projector, he showed his series of "horse in motion" pictures in a machine he had invented called a "zoopraxiscope." It looked like a cake tin with slits in the sides, and the pictures were stuck inside. If you looked through the slits and set the tin spinning, the pictures raced by so fast they merged into a sequence. It really looked as though the horse was moving. Try it yourself at home!

The Scottish inventor William Dickson built a sort of one-man cinema, which he called a "kinetoscope." Through its peephole, just one person could watch a roll of film in motion, which had been taken by a camera also invented by Dickson and called a "kinetograph." In 1894, a kinetoscope salon opened on Broadway in New York City. It was not long before more of these salons opened, including one in Germany.

A big "but," however, had been the fact that there was originally no sound with these first films. Dickson had previously worked for the American inventor Thomas Alva Edison, and during this time they set about solving the problem by providing salons with phonographs, which could record and play sounds. Already on December 24, 1877, Edison submitted his patent for this "talking machine." That's right—inventors don't even stop working on holidays!

William Dickson

Today, movies are lavish productions that can cost a fortune because of special effects, computer animation, or the fees paid to the actors. Two of the most expensive movies ever made are *Pirates of the Caribbean: At World's End* (ca. USD 370 million) and *Spider-Man* (ca. USD 286 million).

Cinematographic techniques have continued to develop, and nowadays we take it for granted that we can watch a movie whenever we like, whether it's at a movie theater or at home.

COMPUTER

You'll find them everywhere today, even in cars and washing machines. Computers ensure that machines do their job in factories and apps function properly on your smartphone or tablet.

Way back in the nineteenth century, there was a forerunner of the computer. The designer was a British mathematician named Charles Babbage, and he set out to build the first programmed calculating machine. In the 1830s, he designed the Analytical Engine, which was supposed to have been several meters long and high, and would have consisted of tens of thousands of cogwheels, disks, and screws. Babbage had planned to make a steam engine to drive the wheels and gears. Like modern computers, this machine would have stored numerical values and a unit for data processing, and would have made it possible to solve complex mathematical equations.

The first program for the machine was written by the English noblewoman Ada Lovelace. She was a mathematical genius and understood the enormous potential of the analytical machine. She produced a series of punched cards with which the machine would be programmed. This makes her the first computer programmer in the history of the world.

The data were punched into paper, creating a pattern of holes.

Babbage worked on his machine until he died, but he only managed to build one part of it. In fact, it really would have made a great impact: at the time, mathematical tables were still compiled by hand— and you will know for yourself how long such things take to write and how easily mistakes can slip in.

Ada Lovelace

Charles Babbage

Harvard Computers was the name given to a group of women who, from 1877, worked at the observatory of that famous American university. They identified and classified thousands of stars by hand. At the time, these women received little respect and not enough payment for their achievements and for the important discoveries they made. Some of them were extremely talented and strong-willed, and they refused to be discouraged—not even by the fact that women were not allowed to use telescopes but had to work with photographs. One of these women was Henrietta Swan Leavitt, who later became a well-known astronomer.

Henrietta Swan Leavitt

One of the first computers available for people to use at home in the late 1970s was the Commodore PET.

Back to computers: they are machines that work according to the rules of a program. In turn, a program consists of a series of instructions written in a language the computer understands. The American computer scientist Grace Hopper invented a computer language called FLOW-MATIC. This was an important step toward writing a computer program that everyone could understand. Hopper's work led to the development of the programming language COBOL (common business-oriented language). This is still in use today and earned Hopper the nicknames "Grandma Cobol" and "Amazing Grace." Even as a child she had been fascinated by math and technology, and she became a true pioneer in the field of information technology. The term "bug" for software errors is connected to her as well. During the 1940s, a computer that Hopper's team was working with broke down because of a moth. She stuck the dead moth in her logbook and wrote next to it, "First actual case of bug being found." And that is why, nowadays, when we remove faults in a program, we call it "debugging."

Apps (application software) are part of every smartphone. These are programs that make it possible to listen to music, paint pictures, keep a diary, write to others, film videos, and play games.

```
0024
0025   PROCEDURE...
0026   TESTING-COBOL
0027        I FUNCTION REVERSE (ST
                    NON-BUL 1 6
       COMPUTE  BT-JOS-LENTE
       DISPLAY BT-THO
       MOVE 1- I
```

Grace Hopper

A tablet is, in principle, the same as a smartphone but bigger. There are certain games that are specially programmed for tablets and in which, for example, you can steer an automobile by moving the tablet.

WORLD WIDE WEB

FROM 1989

Thanks to the World Wide Web, we have access to the contents of the internet. It's a gigantic network of information about virtually any subject you can think of.

The British computer scientist Tim Berners-Lee invented the Word Wide Web (WWW). He was working on the idea of simplifying ways of communicating with other scientists so that they could pool their research on the internet. In order to do this, he designed what is known as HTML (Hypertext Markup Language)— a language that computers can read and use to produce digital documents, such as the first websites that were put on the internet. The WWW is composed of many different HTML documents. It was important for Berners-Lee that every document could link up worldwide with every other document—just like a web. Hence the name World Wide Web. As it was the WWW that made everyone familiar with the internet, many people use the term when they really mean the internet, which in fact is quite different. To make this clearer, emails and the WWW are both services provided by the internet itself, which is a worldwide computer network dating back to 1969. In that year, the research department of the U.S. Department of Defense created a network called ARPANET (Advanced Research Projects Agency Network) for all its military computers. Soon afterwards, universities used more networks as a way of sharing information.

If we were to try to put a date on Berners-Lee's invention, there are several days to choose from. One might say March 12, 1989, because that was the day on which he first proposed the system for information management, which provided the basis for his WWW. He was then working for CERN (the Conseil Européen pour la Recherche Nucléaire, or European Organization for Nuclear Research) in Geneva. Or the date could be December 1990, which is when he succeeded in setting up the first website and the first browser.

Berners-Lee thought his invention should be available for everyone to use. He saw access to the WWW as an electronic right.

Tim Berners-Lee

In 2004, Queen Elizabeth II bestowed a knighthood on Berners-Lee, and since then many people have called him "Sir Tim"...

Berners-Lee came up with alternative names for the WWW, for example, The Information Mine (TIM) and Mine of Information (MOI). Another he considered was Information Mesh.

FREQUENCY HOPPING

Today we can sit in our yards and ask a search engine "What can I play today?" without our laptop needing a wire to connect it to the internet. This is all thanks to an invention by Hedy Lamarr and George Antheil.

When they came up with their invention, though, neither of them was thinking of laptops or smartphones, but of submarines and torpedoes (underwater weapons with their own engine and explosive charge). The extremely complex process that they designed is the basis of modern technologies such as Bluetooth and WLAN.

Born in Austria, Lamarr experienced a variety of exciting events during her life. As a 19-year-old actress she appeared naked in a film that also contained a love

Pope Pius XI

Hedy Lamarr

When Lamarr left her husband, she looked not only for a new life but also for a new name. Her real name when she married was Hedwig Eva Maria Mandl.

scene—no big deal nowadays, but things were very different in 1933. The pope even said that she would go to hell for it.

Lamarr married young, which was not unusual in those days. Her husband was an arms dealer, and so she learned a great deal about weaponry. She accompanied him on his business trips, listened attentively, and thought her own thoughts.

She and her husband were not happy, however, and four years after the wedding, she left him and went first to Paris, then

Bluetooth is a technology that allows for short-range wireless transmission of data, such as music, videos, and pictures, by radio. Two compatible sets can communicate without the need for any cables.

Harald Blåtand

The word Bluetooth comes from the name of a tenth-century king of Denmark and Norway who was called Harald Blåtand (the Danish for "blue tooth"). He is said to have been a very skillful diplomat who succeeded in uniting people, as does Bluetooth. Initially "Bluetooth" was the code name for the technology, but no one could think of anything better, so the name stuck.

33

to London, and later to the U.S. In Hollywood she worked for a well-known film studio and won fame as "the most beautiful woman in the world." But this was not enough for her.

In Hollywood Lamarr met the avant-garde composer Antheil. At that time, the National Socialists were in power in Germany. It was a period of sheer horror, when millions of innocent people were persecuted by the Nazis, lost all their possessions, and in most cases lost their lives as well.

The Second World War had begun in Europe in 1939, and the U.S. had joined the struggle in 1941. The military was looking for a method of directing its long-range missiles (rockets that could fly over thousands of miles).

Suddenly it was extremely fortunate that Lamarr had listened in to all her husband's conversations about weapon technologies. Together with Antheil she developed an idea. The invention that they patented in 1942 used a strip of paper with holes in it similar to the kind used on player-piano rolls.

Lamarr wanted to do something to help the U.S. in the battle against the Nazis.

By "reading" these holes simultaneously, both the sender and receiver could be instructed to change frequency at the same time. The system used seven channels, with the signal jumping from one frequency to another. The reason for these jumps was to prevent the enemy from listening to or interfering with the communications system. Lamarr and Antheil developed their idea into a form of remote control for torpedoes, but at the time no one could have foreseen the potential of their invention.

This was only realized in 1982, when the American physicist Robert Price stumbled across Lamarr and Antheil's patent. The process they had invented to steer torpedoes without any outside interference was also perfect for communications between cell phones, radio networks, and the internet. Toward the end of her life, Lamarr was finally acknowledged as the inventor. Until then, her contribution to the history of technology had received far too little recognition.

George Antheil

Hedy Lamarr

VELCRO

**You only need one hand to open and close Velcro.
The Swiss engineer George de Mestral invented it as
a means of replacing shoelaces and zippers.**

It was lucky that de Mestral had a dog—otherwise, he might never have come up with his invention. When the two of them used to come home from a walk, there were often burrs clinging to the dog's coat. De Mestral examined these little balls under his microscope (which had fortunately been invented!) and saw that they were covered with tiny bristles that could stretch out and then close up again.

At the tips of these bristles were small, flexible hooks. When they came into contact with animal skin or other materials (coats or socks, for example), they clung on. When you pulled them out, generally they didn't break, because the hooks were so pliable.

Nature had got there before the inventor. De Mestral took a strip of nylon (which is very strong) and stuck in some synthetic burrs that also had small, pliable hooks. Then he took a second piece of nylon equipped with tiny loops. The hooks fit into the loops when they were put together. De Mestral called his invention Velcro, a mixture of the French words *velours* (velvet) and *crochet* (hook).

Thanks to their bristles and the help of a dog, the common burr has flown all over the planet and beyond!

George de Mestral

Velcro often travels as far as the Moon.
In order to stop weightless bags of food from flying
around inside the space station, they are held
down by Velcro.

During their leisure time,
the astronauts often play chess:
the pieces are attached to the board
by Velcro to stop them from flying
round the cabin.

Velcro is also useful if an astronaut leaves
the space station and wants to scratch his nose.
There is a piece of Velcro inside the helmet designed
specially for nose scratching, because you can't just
take your helmet off when you're out in space.

One day he received a telephone call. The first men on the Moon, Neil Armstrong and Buzz Aldrin, were wearing his invention! Their space suits were covered with Velcro. Nowadays, it's used on shoes, jackets, and knapsacks, in ships, factories, and space, and also on diapers. When inventions are directly derived from nature—like de Mestral's Velcro—we call the technique "bionics." The term is a combination of "biology" and "technics." In many bathrooms you can hang your towel on hooks that are fixed to the wall with suckers. This invention is derived from the suckers on the tentacles of octopuses. Can you think of other examples?

Whitcomb Judson

ZIPPER

FROM 1851

Thanks to the zipper, we can do up our jackets in an instant and pack things securely in our bags. It can even help to save lives: for firefighters, it's particularly important to get dressed at top speed.

The American inventor Whitcomb Judson got bored with tying up his shoelaces, and so he started to think about something that could be used instead of laces, which were the common fastener during the nineteenth century. He developed the "clasp locker"—two metal chains with a sliding lock—which he also used to fasten clothing. Apparently, however, these chains sometimes clamped together so tightly that pincers were needed to pull them apart—not very practical!

But that often happens: not every invention is an immediate success. In the early 1900s the Swedish-American electrical engineer Gideon Sundback came up with the idea of putting the teeth of the fastener much closer together than in the first models. This made the invention a success, because it was easier to slide the fastener up and down, and from then on, the zipper held together far more efficiently. The same principle is still used today.

Nowadays, zippers are even used on astronauts' space suits.

And there are fireproof zippers on firefighters' uniforms.

Waterproof zippers are practical for diving suits and anoraks.

JEANS

Nowadays almost everybody has a pair of jeans in their closet. They were invented by a German-American businessman named Levi Strauss, who is said to have never worn them himself.

Strauss was born in south Germany in 1829, and his first name then was Löb. His father's business was in textiles and everything connected with sewing. Strauss was just 16 when his father fell ill and died. Together with his mother, Strauss took the brave decision to leave the Bavarian village where the family lived and moved to New York City, where two of his older brothers had

All the gold diggers bought waist overalls from Strauss.

Levi Strauss

During the 1990s, excavations in the U.S. unearthed a pair of jeans that were 115 years old— probably the oldest in the world.

opened a dry-goods business a few years earlier. Strauss had to leave most of his belongings in Bavaria, because passengers were only allowed to take one case aboard the ship that was to carry them across the Atlantic. Strauss liked New York and soon settled down. However, his first name was difficult for Americans to pronounce, so he changed it to Levi.

When gold was first discovered in California in 1848, many people's main aim in life was to find some and get rich quick! Once again, Strauss took a brave decision—and a clever one. He packed his bags and set off for the west coast of the U.S., just like the gold hunters. But he wasn't looking for gold. He and his brothers had come up with a plan: gold miners needed clothes. And so the Strauss family went to San Francisco, where they opened a shop that specialized in work clothes. Strauss came up with a brand new design—you might call it the grand-parent of the jeans we know today. He called them "waist overalls," because they only covered the lower half of the body. They were made of very strong, practical blue material and became popular not only with the gold hunters but also mine workers and farmers.

The material was extremely hard-wearing, and thanks to the blue color (called "indigo"), if they got dirty, it was barely visible.

The fact that Strauss himself had no jeans in his wardrobe was simply because, in those days, it was normal for a businessman to wear a suit. These days, you will see businessmen and even politicians wearing jeans. Would Strauss ever have dreamt that would happen?

In former times, jeans would eventually wear thin because of work. Today, anyone who wants a pair of jeans that look threadbare can buy them with all the appropriate holes and tears already there.

41

SOCCER BOOTS

When he was still a teenager, the German cobbler and inventor Adi Dassler kept thinking to himself that there ought to be special shoes for every kind of sport—for example, soccer, so that people could play the game in all weathers.

When Dassler was 19, he decided that he would make these shoes himself. He was not put off by the fact that he was living in difficult times (the First World War had just ended). As a great fan of soccer, football, athletics, and boxing, he was determined to design appropriate footwear for each sport. He set up a workshop in the shed his mother had used for her laundry business, and he proved to have a highly inventive mind. In order to earn the money for his materials, he mended shoes. He also collected used boots from the military in order to reuse the leather.

During the decades that followed, he and his brother Rudolf established a company that even supplied shoes to participants in the Olympic Games. Many years later,

The first orders have arrived! Sending sample soccer boots to the clubs has paid off.

Rudolf Dassler

Adi Dassler

Today, professional soccer players may use 40 to 50 pairs of boots in a single season.

the brothers decided to go their separate ways, and each of them founded their own sports equipment company: Adi's became Adidas, and Rudolf's was Puma.

During the 1950s, Adi was made an adviser to the German soccer team and was known as "the shoemaker of the nation." Before every game, he advised the team on the best choice of boots to suit the weather and the condition of the pitch.

In 1954, the final of the World Cup in Switzerland was between West Germany and the hot favorites, Hungary. Conditions were bad, because the pitch was extremely wet and slippery. Dassler had a brilliant idea: at halftime he screwed longer studs into the soles of the players' boots. This stopped them from constantly slipping and sliding, whereas the mud stuck to the Hungarians' shorter studs, which made their boots heavier—and with heavy boots you can't run as fast. The German team came from behind to win 3–2, and the match went down in history as "the miracle of Bern."

Over time, not only the boots but also clothing has undergone major changes—especially for women! In the nineteenth century, they still wore hats and short skirts over pants.

FIZZ

When we talk of fizz, we usually mean the little bubbles of gas in sparkling mineral water and fizzy drinks. What sparkles is actually a gas with no color and no smell.

Jacob Schweppe

Joseph Priestley

Thomas Henry

Fizz is carbonic acid (H_2CO_3), which is the combination of water (H_2O) and a gas named carbon dioxide (CO_2). If you boil the water, the bubbles will disappear. At first, the invention of fizz was only for mineral water and not for any other drinks. The addition of carbon dioxide helps it keep for longer. Water containing minerals was used as a medicine during the nineteenth century, so in those days, fizz allowed pharmacists to store medicine for longer before they sold it. Carbon dioxide ensures that the minerals in the water remain stable. Several inventors contributed their ideas to making mineral water last longer.

In the early 1770s, the British chemists Joseph Priestley and Thomas Henry, independently of each other, found ways of incorporating carbon dioxide in water. Priestley's main interest was

Sometimes you get a tickly feeling when you drink water or lemonade containing carbon dioxide. When the drink reaches your stomach, the gas tries to find its way out—this is what makes you belch.

There is also natural fizzy water—that is, it contains natural carbon dioxide—especially in regions where there were once active volcanoes. Carbonic acid also has a practical quality: it helps to release minerals from rocks.

research into gases—he is also the person who discovered nitrous oxide, which became known as laughing gas. This can be used for dental treatment or operations, to help the patient relax.

From 1780, the Geneva-based jeweler and clockmaker Jacob Schweppe also worked on a method of adding carbon dioxide to water. He soon noticed that even healthy people enjoyed drinking his fizzy water. Schweppe decided to build a factory in order to mass-produce it, and his products became extremely successful. In 1836, his company even received a royal warrant from the British royal family.

TOOTHPASTE

If you don't forget to clean your teeth—and you'd better not!—then in all likelihood, toothpaste will be the first and last taste of your day.

In 1850, when he was 23 years old, Washington Sheffield invented toothpaste. At that time, it was customary to clean your teeth with a powder bought from the pharmacist. This was a mixture of pumice stone, powdered marble, grated oyster shells, ashes, peppermint oil or sage, and some soap powder. How do you think that would have tasted? In the nineteenth century it was seen as especially stylish to mix something red in with the other ingredients, because red lips were regarded as particularly beautiful.

What was special about Sheffield's idea was the addition of glycerin. This was mixed with the powder to create a paste, which was packed in bags of tinfoil. However, this proved impractical, as it quickly dried up because the bags had to be cut open and could not be closed again. While Sheffield's son was studying in Paris, he noticed that artists squeezed their paint out of tubes, and it occurred to him that toothpaste could also be packed in tubes. He passed the idea on to his father. Nowadays, toothpaste comes in various forms, with stripes and many different flavors. You can also clean your teeth with tooth powder or with tablets that you chew.

Washington Sheffield

The pharaohs of ancient Egypt cleaned their teeth with "chew sticks" and pastes made from wine vinegar, crushed pumice stone, or the semiprecious stone malachite.

Prehistoric humans also cleaned their teeth. This was discovered when archaeologists' excavations uncovered bones and teeth dating back to the Stone Age. There were grooves in the teeth that had been caused by sticks that were almost certainly used to brush and clean between teeth.

A healthy tooth is encased in enamel— the hardest substance in the body. However, a sticky film known as plaque can build up on the teeth and destroy the enamel. With toothpaste, you can brush away the film and prevent decay and inflammation of your gums.

Crocodiles have live toothbrushes: little birds come and peck remaining bits of meat out of their mouths. Cleaner fish swim into the open mouths of sharks and take out the leftovers without being eaten themselves. In contrast, anteaters don't have any teeth, so they don't need to do any cleaning!

INSTANT NOODLES

Momofuku Andō changed the way we eat when he invented instant noodles. Not only do they keep for ever and a day, but they can be prepared in less than three minutes.

Instant noodles are most often made from wheat flour, salt, water, and spices. They're produced by being precooked and then dipped in hot oil. The heat removes the water from the noodles, after which they are packed in airtight plastic bags.

Andō hated to see people starving: that was the inspiration for his invention. It all started in 1945, when the Second World War came to an end. Japan surrendered on August 15, an especially memorable day for Andō. He lived in Osaka, where many homes had been destroyed by bombs. He saw people standing in a long line in front of one of the damaged houses, waiting for a bowl of noodles,

For many Japanese people, the invention of instant noodles is one of the country's great success stories. But there are different opinions as to how healthy they really are.

麺

Andō even developed instant noodles for space travel, working together with the Japanese space agency JAXA ...

which were being cooked in large pots. Then it suddenly occurred to him: it must be possible to prepare noodles much more quickly.

There followed years of experimenting and testing. Andō founded his own company in 1948, and a good 10 years later, he at last found the magic formula. The first chicken-flavored instant noodles were made and sold.

Today, billions of what are now known as pot noodles are made and sold every year. There is a wide range of flavors, including duck, beef, and shrimp. It was Andō's dream to end hunger all over the world. He once said: "Peace will come to the world when people have enough to eat."

... The Japanese astronaut Soichi Noguchi tried them out when he took part in a mission aboard the U.S. space shuttle Discovery in 2005. His verdict? Delicious.

The first flavor for instant noodles was Chikin Ramen (chicken).

Momofuku Andō

Making instant noodles is super simple:

ICE CREAM MAKER

In the old days, you needed strong arms to make ice cream. Nowadays it's simple. And you can also get ice cream in all kinds of flavors, from strawberry and pumpkin-seed nougat to fish!

Nancy Johnson must have loved ice cream, because she had a good idea: she put a hand crank in a little churn. With the aid of this mechanical whisk, she could quickly stir the milk and other ingredients into a creamy mass and her arms felt fine! Inside the churn was a cylinder for the mixing, and all around it Johnson packed crushed ice that Mother Nature had provided. She was granted a patent for this invention.

When the ice cream was ready, it had to be eaten straight away, because in Johnson's day there were no refrigerators or freezers. Ice was collected in winter from lakes and rivers, and in order to prevent it from melting in the summer, people used to store the blocks in wooden crates down in cool cellars. Johnson's ice cream maker underwent an important development in 1906, when the machine was equipped with an electric motor to do the stirring. Another major advance came in the 1930s, with the introduction of cool compressors, which chill the mixture as it's being churned—a technique that is still in use today.

With a refrigerator, a gaseous coolant is pumped through a long, thin, winding metal pipe that runs both outside and inside it. The gas is first compressed by a pump on the outside, causing its pressure and temperature to rise. It then passes through the exterior part of the pipe, where it loses some of its heat to the surrounding air. The pressure is lowered again, causing the gas to become cold before it is piped through the inside of the refrigerator, cooling it and its contents down. This technology is important not only to prevent food from going bad but also to preserve medicines and vaccines.

Nancy Johnson

In Japan there are some special varieties of ice cream: hicken, onion, shrimp, spinach, goat meat ... All of these varieties contain butter, milk, and sugar, and—depending on the flavor—soy sauce, seaweed, meat, fish, or vegetables.

At the end of the thirteenth century, Marco Polo reported eating a mixture of rice pudding and frozen milk, which he had discovered in China. It is believed that this is how the idea of making ice cream first found its way to Italy.

The Roman emperor Nero ate crushed ice mixed with raspberries, cinnamon, ginger, and rosewater. It was not very different from the sorbets that we eat today.

If you suddenly get a pain in your brain while you're eating ice cream—otherwise known as brain freeze—push your tongue up against the roof of your mouth. The warmth will help the blood vessels to relax and the pain will go away.

The tallest ice cream cone in the world was made in Norway in 2015. It was 10 feet, 1.26 inches (3.08 meters) high and had to be transported from the ice cream factory by helicopter, hanging from a rope.

As long as 5,000 years ago, the Chinese used snow and natural ice to cool their drinks. They stored it in dark cellars deep underground, to keep it from melting for as long as possible.

AQUARIUM

FROM 1832

As long ago as the tenth century, the Chinese kept goldfish in porcelain tubs as pets. About 900 years later, a French marine biologist built glass tanks in order to study sea creatures.

Jeanne Villepreux grew up in a French village. Her father was a shoemaker, and the sea was a long way away. When she was 18, she moved to Paris and became a dressmaker. She was so talented that she was even asked to design a wedding dress for a princess. After Villepreux got married, she and her husband moved to Sicily, an Italian island in the Mediterranean Sea, where she stopped sewing and instead devoted herself to research. In 1832, she built glass and wooden tanks into which she pumped seawater—these were the first aquariums. She also constructed wooden cages to lower into the sea so that she could more closely observe the cephalopods, such as squid, cuttlefish, and octopuses, that would take up residence in them.

Her invention has helped scientists to study sea creatures at close quarters, which is only possible if the observation post fits in with the animals' natural environment. And tourists can also enjoy the experience. Another important use of aquariums is different types of research. For instance, by studying the genome of zebra fish we can learn much about our own genome: about 70 percent of this fish's genes are similar to ours.

The blobfish lives deep down in the sea. It has a jelly-like body and its head looks like a goblin's might.

Villepreux discovered that female argonauts—a type of octopus—can grow a new shell if their original one gets broken.

With 71 percent of the Earth lying under water, there is still plenty left to explore!

Jeanne Villepreux

The largest public aquarium in the world is in China. Its biggest tank contains more than 6 million U.S. gallons (23 million liters) of water.

53

FIRE EXTINGUISHER

Many things have been saved thanks to the invention of the fire extinguisher: homes, offices, factories, and most importantly, human lives.

Already 2,000 years ago, romans used water spray guns, which were able to shoot over 98 feet (30 meters).

About 200 years ago, superstitious people still believed they could put out a fire through rituals, such as by throwing wooden plates into the flames and muttering magic spells.

Early in the nineteenth century, the British engineer George William Manby witnessed a terrible accident at sea. It affected him so badly that he decided to invent things that would save human lives. He not only thought of the sea and its dangers, for which he worked on a kind of lifeboat, but he also invented a fire extinguisher. He used potassium carbonate to put out the flames—a powder that used to be extracted from the ashes of plants and can be used for all kinds of things, including the manufacture of soap.

Not all early fire extinguishers were successful. Nature gave the engineer W. C. Philipp the idea that he could put

George William Manby

out fires with steam released under pressure from a fire extinguisher: during a voyage at sea, he had observed how a volcanic eruption formed steam over the sea and put out a fire on a nearby island. However, after the British inventor's own factory burned down in 1856, there were no more customers for his fire extinguisher.

In 1872, the American inventor Thomas J. Martin designed an extinguisher that could be attached to a water tank so that it could draw on large quantities of water.

Today there are different kinds of extinguisher on the market, using water, powder, foam, or carbon dioxide, which smothers the flames. Of course, there are professionals who do the job. Find out when the fire station in your area is holding an open day and go along: you'll learn all there is to know about fires and how to extinguish them.

W. C. Philipp

Thomas J. Martin

There were once some supposedly miraculous (and extremely expensive) fire extinguishers that were filled with solutions and salts, and gave off impressive hissing and steaming sounds, but they never did much more than that.

PLASTIC

The word "plastic" is a colloquial term for any synthetic material. It is derived from the Greek *plastikós*, which means "malleable" (you can shape it to any form). Its special feature is that even a tiny change in the formula can have a major effect on the product.

Leo Hendrik Baekeland

The forerunner of plastic was casein. Wolfgang Seidel, a monk who lived in Augsburg, south Germany, discovered that he could make a material out of low-fat cheese. It could be shaped while it was warm, and when it cooled it remained extremely solid. For this to happen, it needed to be warmed and cooled several times, but he was able to make cups and even jewelry out of it.

According to how much heat and pressure is applied, and regardless of whether other materials are added or not, the product can be a plastic bottle, a toy, or even a piece of medical equipment used to save lives. The inventor of the first mass-produced and completely synthetic material was the Belgian chemist Leo Hendrik Baekeland. He called his invention Bakelite. In order to produce it, he mixed phenol and formaldehyde together and heated them in a pressure vessel to almost 392° Fahrenheit (200° Celsius). His invention set off a gigantic wave of development in synthetic materials.

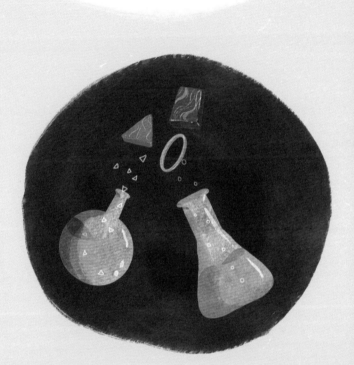

Synthetic materials can be made from crude oil. This is found below the surface of the Earth and has to be pumped out. When it's refined, it's separated into liquid and gas, plus residue. These components have to be heated in chemical factories and processed under pressure. Oil is a natural raw material, which means that its supply is not unlimited.

The different types of plastic can be divided into three groups. There are thermoplastics, which become soft when heated and hard again when they cool (*thermos* is the Greek for "warm"). PET (polyethylene terephthalate) bottles, which are commonly used for water and fruit juices, belong to this category. Duromers (from the Latin *durare*, meaning "to last" or "to harden") cannot be softened once they have been molded. These include phenoplasts, which many everyday items are made of, such as lamps and the handles of pots and pans. And the third category is elastomers (from the Greek *elastós*, meaning "expandable"), which are not solid but malleable. The raw material of chewing gum is one example.

Baekeland had invented something of major importance. However, we now know that plastic waste can cause enormous damage. Imagine: a single PET bottle can take 450 years to decompose, and even then, little pieces of plastic still survive. Every minute, about 10 million plastic bags are being used all over the world. Countless tons of plastic waste have found their way into the oceans over the past few decades—and this is still going on. Every year up to 135,000 whales are caught up in mountains of plastic waste, and it's certain that millions of seabirds, fish, and other marine creatures eat bits of plastic thinking that they are food. Many have died because of it. Between 1950 and 2015, 8.3 billion metric tons of plastic were produced worldwide. Most of this was used for disposable products and packaging. Not even 10 percent was recycled. Some governments have therefore started to regulate the use of plastic, and more and more people, especially environmentalists, are going to great lengths to determine exactly where it is really necessary to use these materials,

Some companies are fishing plastics out of the sea and, if possible, reusing them. For example, gym shoes and knapsacks are being made out of plastic items recovered from the oceans.

where we can eliminate them altogether, and how we can use eco-friendly raw materials to produce new synthetic ones.

The toy company Lego, for instance, has been doing research for several years on a plastic-free way of manufacturing its bricks. It expects to be shifting to eco-friendly materials by 2030. In recent years, "zero waste" movements have sprung up in many towns, with people making every effort to end pollution caused by plastic bags, bottles, and straws.

You can find raw plastic in chewing gum.

FLYING MACHINES

Otto Lilienthal

When you think of airplanes, you probably picture machines with lots of seats, big wings, and jet engines. The fact that all these exist has a great deal to do with Otto Lilienthal, "the flying man."

If you imagine the history of flight as being a long road, Lilienthal is unquestionably right at the beginning of it, and he laid the first foundations with his flying of gliders. These taught him a great deal about aerodynamics—a science that concerns itself with air resistance, air currents, and how bodies react up in the air. Lilienthal gleaned his ideas for flying machines from his studies of nature. He was particularly fascinated by the construction of birds' wings. Even as a child, Lilienthal loved watching storks and gulls, and as a 14 year old, he tried to fly. His main preoccupation was the problem of takeoff: how does something that is heavier than air manage to get up into the air and stay there? A few years later, he conducted his own experiments, hanging from a rope from the roof of his family

Flying squirrels are talented gliders, as are flying fish. The latter catapult themselves out of the water and can glide up to 1,300 feet (400 meters) at a speed of up to 43 miles (70 kilometers) per hour.

Four of Lilienthal's Normalsegelapparats have survived. One of them is in the Science Museum in London, and another is in the collection of the National Air and Space Museum in Washington, D.C.

In 1989, the British hang glider Judy Leden had herself lifted on a line by a hot-air balloon high above the south coast of England. As she went over the white cliffs of Dover, she detached herself from the line and became the first woman to fly across the English Channel with a hang glider.

Judy Leden

home, wearing a wing-beating apparatus—he really looked as if he had birds' wings, even if he couldn't fly with them!

When he grew up, Lilienthal lived in Berlin and he kept four storks in his garden. He observed them closely to see if the flight technology could be transferred to people. Birds' bones, however, are much lighter than humans', and so in order to achieve liftoff, a human would need a huge wingspan and enormous muscle power. Therefore, Lilienthal had to accept that imitating the birds would not get him very far. With the aid of detailed drawings and complex mathematical formulas concerning length and weight, he designed what we would now call a "paraglider." He found that slightly curved wing surfaces increased the capacity for flight. He went on to build several different models, including double-deckers and wing-beating gliders. Over and over again, he jumped off hills in order to test his models. From a nearby hill, he eventually managed a flight of 82 feet (25 meters). From 1894, he flew with a single-decker glider that had a

wingspan of 22 feet (6.7 meters). With this he accomplished flights of up to 820 feet (250 meters). In order to carry out these experiments, he had a "flight hill" built near his home that was almost 50 feet (15 meters) high. He went on to make these gliders—called Normalsegelapparats—to order, and so one might say that he was the first person in history to mass-produce a flying machine. The price at the time was 500 deutsche marks, which is about USD 4,000 in today's currency.

Sadly, Lilienthal did not enjoy his success for very long. On August 9, 1896, he crashed from a height of 49 feet (15 meters) during one of his test flights and was badly injured. He died in hospital in Berlin the following day.

In 2004, Angelo d'Arrigo flew a hang glider, without any additional oxygen, over the high peak of Mount Everest (29,035 feet; 8,850 meters). The wind speed was up to 125 miles (200 kilometers) per hour and the temperature was -58° Fahrenheit (-50° Celsius).

AIRPLANE

For centuries people dreamed of being able to fly. The American inventors Orville and Wilbur Wright made this dream come true. They built the first airplane with steering and its own engine.

Orville Wright

Wilbur Wright

WRIGHT CYCLE CO

The Wright brothers were full of enthusiasm when they heard about Otto Lilienthal's gliders, and they were determined to build their own flying machine. They began with a hang glider. There soon followed double-decker gliders that could carry one person, and they went on to design and test other forms of flight. They even mounted testing apparatus on a bicycle and then pedaled as fast as they could along the road in order to create the sort of air current they might encounter during a flight.

They were particularly keen to develop a three-axis control system for their flying machine so that, unlike Lilienthal's gliders, it would not be at the mercy of the winds. In 1901 they made an important advance: they designed a sideways rudder that enabled them to steer to the left and to the right. One year later, they had completed the

The Wright brothers moved to a small town on the east coast of the U.S. The wind on the seashore was useful for their flight experiments. Until then, they had only owned a bicycle workshop.

Two propellers drove the machine from the rear.

The plane had runners instead of rollers and slid along a short wooden rail before it took off.

The double-decker, one-man Flyer I, with its white wings, was powered by a four-cylinder, gasoline-driven engine of 12 horsepower.

The pilot lay on his stomach, right next to the engine on the lower wing, and steered the machine from there.

steering design: now they could raise and lower the nose of the machine so that it could go up or down. The brothers then designed an engine to drive the propeller. Neither of them had any training in machine construction, but their ingenuity and technical skills helped them, and in 1903 they were ready with their first powered machine, the Flyer I. On December 17 of that year, Orville flew 120 feet (37 meters) along the shore—little more than a big jump in the air that only lasted about 12 seconds. However, on the same day the brothers made three more flights, the last of which is believed to have covered 852 feet (259 meters). In 1905, Flyer III flew almost 25 miles (40 kilometers). In 1908, for the first time, the Flyer had a passenger on board.

Jet engines burn an enormous amount of fuel and produce a tremendously powerful thrust. The modern Boeing 777 has two engines that propel the aircraft with 175,000 horsepower.

Two years later, the brothers went on a test flight, which was the first time they had flown together—and they asked their father beforehand for his permission. They had previously always promised him that, because of the enormous risks involved in flying, they would only ever fly one at a time. They subsequently founded a company to mass-produce their flying machines. It is because of their inventions that all of us can fly like birds high in the sky.

Amelia Earhart was the first woman to fly solo across the Atlantic, and was the first person to cross the Pacific between Hawaii and California. She died while attempting to fly the length of the equator around the Earth. During the final stage, she was unable to receive any radio signals and couldn't find the island on which she wanted to land. As many as 64 planes and eight warships were sent to look for her, but they never found her.

In 1909, a pilot named John Moore-Brabazon took a pig with him on a flight. It was a joke to indicate that the impossible is possible: pigs can fly! The pig was called Icarus II, and it landed safely back on Earth—unlike its namesake in Greek mythology.

Pilots train for many hours in a flight simulator.

Harriet Quimby was the first woman to be given a pilot's license in the U.S., and in 1912 she became the first woman to fly solo across the English Channel.

Amelia Earhart

Harriet Quimby

Leonardo da Vinci, painter, sculptor, musician, philosopher, engineer, and natural scientist, would no doubt have rejoiced to see the motor-powered aircraft, because way back in the fifteenth century he himself had designed a flying machine with a propeller—a kind of great-great-grandfather to the helicopter.

Thanks to their modern jet engines, airplanes can now fly all over the world in a relatively short time. Jumbo jets can carry up to 850 passengers. Aircraft also transport vast quantities of freight. But all this causes a great deal of damage to the environment: the burning fuel produces carbon dioxide, and this warms the climate. The harmful effects of this are being felt all over our planet. That is why, among other things, research scientists are working to develop new kinds of fuel.

LETTERPRESS PRINTING

The German goldsmith Johannes Gutenberg's invention of the printing press opened up new worlds for large numbers of people. Texts could now be widely distributed, which brought about great changes to science, religion, and culture.

The printed paper was hung up to dry, like washing on a line, because it had to absorb the wet print.

NEWS

Johannes Gutenberg

Before Gutenberg invented the printing press, books had to be copied by hand. This made them extremely expensive, because it required a great deal of time and effort. Try doing it with just a couple of pages and then imagine if you had to copy hundreds of them! In China, Japan, Korea, and other Asian countries, we know that print with carved wooden blocks was already in use from the seventh century, but this method also took a lot of time, because the text and picture for one page had to be carved by hand into each block.

Gutenberg's talents as a goldsmith were very useful when it came to

The letters could be used over and over again. When the printing was finished, they only had to be taken apart from each other and then put together again.

Thanks to Gutenberg's invention, the very first newspaper was printed in Strasbourg as early as 1605.

making a printing press. He was able to produce different forms of letters, such as upper- and lowercase. He could put these together to create words, then separate them again and store them in a box. In order to make the letters, he used a hollow mold into which he poured a mixture of lead and other metals.

The invention of the printing press was a technological revolution. Because it was now much easier to produce books, more and more people learned to read and were able to find out about a great variety of subjects. For centuries, very few people had been able to read, and so they had the power to decide what information should be distributed and how history should be presented to the rest of the world. Thanks to Gutenberg's invention, the ability to learn other languages and study different subjects was no longer limited to the very rich. During the following century, many millions of books were printed throughout the world. This seems a lot, but it was nothing compared to the number of books that exist today. Did you know that more than 500 million copies of the *Harry Potter* books have been sold worldwide?

The heaviest book in the world is *The Book of the Apocalypse*, a work of art created between 1958 and 1961 with the participation of the Spanish artist Salvador Dalí. It has 300 pages of large-format parchment and weighs 463 pounds (210 kilograms), which is as heavy as a full-grown male lion!

Salvador Dalí

In total, 180 *Gutenberg Bibles* were printed, and 49 of them still exist today.

For a long time, traditional fairy tales were only handed down orally. This was changed by two German brothers named Grimm. Thanks to the invention of the printing press, the first volume of *Children's and Household Tales* was published in Berlin in 1812. It contained 86 stories, including *Sleeping Beauty* and *Hansel and Gretel*.

The first printed bestseller in history was the two-volume *Gutenberg Bible*, which contains almost 1,300 pages. It is also known as the B42, because each page was printed with two columns of 42 lines each.

The famous American writer Mark Twain said Gutenberg's invention was "incomparably the mightiest event that has ever happened in profane history."

This is J.K. Rowling, the creator of *Harry Potter*.

The Tales of Beedle the Bard is another book written by the British writer J. K. Rowling. Initially, only seven copies were produced and each was handwritten and illustrated by Rowling herself; the printed version first came out a year later. One of the handwritten versions was bought for almost USD 4 million at an auction, with the money going to a children's charity! The tales in this book are familiar to every magical child in the world of *Harry Potter*—though they were not to Harry and Hermione, of course, as they grew up with muggles.

BRAILLE

FROM 1825

With six dots, 16-year-old Louis Braille changed the world. He invented a form of writing for blind people that enabled them to read and write.

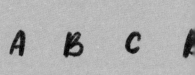

A B C

Braille organized six dots, as on a dice. The simplest letter—"a"—is one dot at the top left.

Louis Braille

Braille's life story begins with a bad accident. When he was three, he stabbed himself in the eye with one of his father's tools by mistake. The injury became infected, and not long afterwards, the infection spread to the other eye, with the result that, by the age of five, Braille was completely blind. But he was very strong-willed and did not want to be shut out from life as he had known it. His father made him some wooden blocks with nails in that were arranged in the form of letters. With these, his parents taught him the alphabet. At that time, one of the first special schools for the blind was in Paris, and Braille was given a place there when he was 10.

The blind children learned mainly by listening to and repeating what the teacher said. This was called the "parrot" method, and it was heavy going! When Braille was 11, a visitor came to the school. His name was Charles Barbier and he was a soldier. He told the children about his invention of a special form of writing that soldiers had been using to send each other secret messages.

R S T

Charles Barbier

This is Barbier's "night writing," which inspired Braille to invent his alphabet for the blind.

He also developed combinations of dots for mathematical symbols and musical notes. Braille was able to convince his headmaster that his alphabet worked, and his fellow students greeted it with great enthusiasm.

In 1878, it was decided by experts in the field that this form of writing should be used officially in schools for the blind. Today, braille is used all over the world to write different languages, numbers, musical notes, and chemical and mathematical formulas. Sometimes the dots can mean different things: for instance, the combination for the German "ch" is used for "th" in English texts, as well as for a "T" sound in Arabic and Hebrew. Braille is to be found on bank and insurance cards, and of course in books, including *The Gruffalo* and *Harry Potter and the Philosopher's Stone*, which are larger and thicker in braille than conventional editions.

He called it "night writing" and explained that it consisted of raised dots imprinted on paper that represented letters and syllables that you could identify by touch. This enabled soldiers to read during the night without anyone else knowing and without having to light a lantern. This gave Braille the idea of using dots to create a form of writing that blind people could read with their fingers.

Just a few years later, he had devised an alphabet for the blind using six dots. It was an ingenious system: the dots could be combined in 64 different ways to create letters and numbers.

Today you can feel braille on packets of medicine.

POST-ITS

Art Fry sang in a choir. He needed to mark different pages of his songbook, and so he would put bits of paper in it, but these kept falling out.

This gave Fry the idea of making little notelets that would stick but could also be easily removed. Fry was a chemistry technician in the research department of a large American company. He remembered that his research colleague Spencer Silver had worked on an extra-strong glue in 1968. Silver had succeeded in developing a glue that stuck to almost all surfaces, but not so strong that the items couldn't easily be separated. Fry realized that this glue would be perfect for his notelets and bookmarks. He improved the glue so that it could stick to paper and be peeled off afterwards without tearing the page or leaving little remnants on it.

Initially there wasn't a choice of colors: Post-its were bright yellow (and often still are). This came about because, when the notelets were being invented, the nearest laboratory only had yellow scrap paper available—it was simply a matter of chance!

Today there are Post-its in pastel and neon shades, and in the shape of hearts, speech bubbles, and arrows.

Art Fry

Spencer Silver

However, Fry was unable to convince the head of his company, who dismissed the notelets as just sticky pieces of paper. This was a disappointment, but he didn't give up. Fry and the head of his department used the sticky notes on short messages, plans, and documents that they sent each other. And in the end, Fry was able to get even the big boss to change his mind. In order to convince the heads of other companies how practical this idea was, people were trained to go and explain how these Post-its could be used. Many found the invention very useful, and it now ranks as one of the most popular inventions of the twentieth century. The notes are used in more than a hundred countries.

Imagine: every year so many Post-its are produced that if you stuck them all next to each other, they would cover more than 6.2 million miles (10 million kilometers). With this quantity, you could stick a path to the Moon and back several times over!

The production of Post-its begins with a roll of paper some 5.6 miles (9 kilometers) long and 1,764–1,984 pounds (800–900 kilograms) in weight—about as heavy as a polar bear or a leatherback turtle.

The paper is then "painted" with glue and cut into squares of 5 feet (1.5 meters). The notes are then stacked in piles of 100 and cut in the format of Post-it blocks.

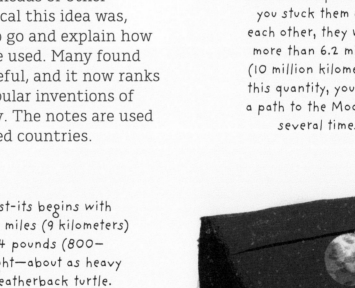

RADIOACTIVITY

Marie Curie discovered radioactive elements and their qualities. In 1903, she became the first woman to receive the most important award in the world of scientific research: the Nobel Prize. Then, it was in physics—and in 1911, she won it again in chemistry.

At the age of four, Marie could already read and solve math problems. When she grew up, she moved from her native Warsaw to Paris. In those days, women were not allowed to study in Poland, but she was not going to let that stop her. In 1891, she began to study physics at the famous university of Sorbonne in Paris. Apart from her, there were just 20 women enrolled at the university, compared to more than 1,800 men. When Marie took her exams, she came top in all her subjects. In 1894, she got to know the physicist Pierre Curie and they fell in love, got married, and from then on always worked together. Marie discovered the previously unknown chemical elements polonium and radium and the nature of their radiation, for which she coined the term "radioactive."

The word "radium" became fashionable, and restaurants and movie theaters were named after the element Marie had discovered.

In 1921, the U.S. president Warren G. Harding presented Marie with one gram of radium after an American journalist had appealed for donations on her behalf. This was worth a huge amount, and it enabled her to continue with her research.

Radioactive rays are invisible and can penetrate solid materials to some extent. You can't feel them, but when materials are charged with radioactivity, the rays are strong enough to make them glow in the dark. The potential of radium as a means of combating cancer soon became a hot topic in the field of research. Throughout her life, Marie was often the first to start or invent things. For instance, she was the first woman in France to teach at a university.

During the First World War, she focused her attention on radiology. She built mobile X-ray machines and equipped 20 "radiological vehicles" with them. These made it possible to see broken bones or bullets in the bodies of wounded soldiers. Many lives were saved, because hospitals were usually a long way away from the battlefields.

Marie Curie

Marie's radiological cars became known as
Little Curies. The inventor even got herself a driving
license so that she could drive them herself.

X-rays are electromagnetic rays.
Their special feature is that they
enable us to see through solid objects.
This was discovered in 1895 by the
German scientist Wilhelm Conrad
Röntgen. He realized that thanks
to these rays, you could see inside
a body—all the bones and organs.

These are X-rays of
an arm and a pelvis.

Together with her daughter Irène, Marie taught other women to work with X-ray machines. Even after the war, radiology continued to play an important role in medicine—as indeed it still does today—and Marie resumed her research on radium. In fact, she never stopped working.

Radium was the most radioactive of all the materials then known. It is also one of the rarest natural elements. Marie died in 1934. The radiation from the elements she had discovered had made her ill. Irène also became a physicist and chemist, and also won a Nobel Prize. She worked on the elements her mother had discovered, and her health also suffered as a consequence. It was probably the cause of her leukemia.

Irène Curie

There are notebooks, sketches, and even a recipe book by Marie. However, they are still so badly irradiated that they can only be touched if you're wearing protective clothing.

MICROSCOPE

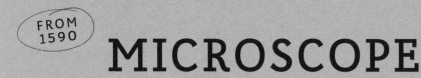

If you look very closely at something, you will understand it better. A microscope enlarges the tiniest object. That's how we can study things that would otherwise be invisible. And there are a lot of those!

Without the invention of the microscope, we would not even know that bacteria exist, and we would never have found out that they can make us ill. Scientists would not have been able to find out about human genetics or how cells divide. All this is important in our efforts to cure illnesses.

The first microscope was made at the end of the sixteenth century. It was then possible to magnify objects up to nine times their real size, and from then on, scientists naturally wanted to see things even more clearly and to make even more discoveries. The Dutch inventor Antonie van Leeuwenhoek succeeded in making things look almost 270 times bigger.

A magnifying glass can make a letter two to six times bigger.

Mikros is the Greek word for "small." "Scope" is derived from skopein, which means "to observe."

Van Leeuwenhoek found bacteria in his dental plaque—he deliberately didn't clean his teeth for a while, but don't tell anyone!

This is what cells and their nuclei look like when seen through a microscope.

This was a huge step. From this, he found out that capillaries (very small blood vessels) exist in living creatures, and that red blood corpuscles move around in frogs' feet. Especially important for science was his discovery of bacteria, for example, in ponds and rainwater, human saliva, and his own dental plaque. This marked the beginning of research into tiny microorganisms— and the discovery of which ones can make us ill.

Dust mites are some of the creatures that we share our homes with, although we can't see them. They become visible under a microscope. They are less than half a millimeter in length, are blind, live in our beds and sofas, and eat their way through the dust. They are not pretty and could well play the part of extraterrestrial monsters in a superhero film.

Van Leeuwenhoek screwed tiny lenses between brass plates.

No one had ever seen this before: Van Leeuwenhoek made an amazing discovery in a pond. What he found looked like little animals. Nobody believed him, but he had discovered bacteria and other single-cell creatures.

Antonie van Leeuwenhoek

These are good bacteria that live in our intestines.

But these intestinal bacte can cause sickness.

The instrument Van Leeuwenhoek used is called a "light microscope," because the enlargement is done with the aid of light. If you look round your school, you'll probably find that light microscopes are being used there, but they're very different from those used in van Leeuwenhoek's time. This is how a light microscope works: an enlarged image of a thin, illuminated object is produced with the aid of the objective lens and light. You look at it through the eyepiece, which functions like a magnifying glass and expands the image even more.

But the light microscope only allows limited enlargement. That is why the French physicist Louis de Broglie looked for a way to enlarge objects still further. In 1924, he discovered that moving electrons—tiny, negatively charged particles of matter—can be used to magnify specimens. These are objects that are prepared for the microscope and often are laid out on wafer-thin glass plates. They might be parts of an insect or a plant. In 1931, the German electronics engineer Ernst Ruska built the electron microscope, which enlarges images by 2 million times! This enabled scientists to study the structures of the tiniest living creatures, including viruses.

With the aid of a special form of light microscope—a STED microscope—you can even study DNA. This is a kind of instruction manual for all parts of the body, and is situated in the nucleus of every cell.

In an electron microscope, an electronic beam is produced. Imagine a superhero firing the beam through the tube of the microscope. When the beam hits the part of the specimen you want to look at, this also radiates electrons, and these are caught by the microscope. And so the beam gradually reaches the whole specimen, bit by bit. The electrons that bounce back and are caught by the microscope combine to form a picture, and this shows the specimen in a greatly enlarged form.

In 2014, the Nobel Prize in Chemistry was awarded to a team of German and American chemists for their high-performance light microscope, which opened the way to studying individual molecules in living cells. One molecule contains multiple atoms. For example, water molecules (H_2O) consist of two hydrogen atoms and one oxygen atom. The chemists were even able to show how molecules move between the nerve cells of the brain, and to observe individual proteins in fertilized eggs.

Louis de Broglie

VACCINATION

Smallpox was a terrible disease that killed millions of people over many centuries. A young doctor invented vaccination—a true lifesaver! And you'll never guess why it wouldn't have been possible without a cow!

As the popular story goes, one day a young milkmaid told the British doctor Edward Jenner that she would never catch the pox. This made him curious. The milkmaid apparently explained to Jenner that she had already caught cowpox from her cow and this had made her immune to any other form of pox. "Immune" means that the body becomes insensitive to the causes of certain illnesses. Humans could be infected by cowpox, but it was not dangerous. (It rarely happens, but even today it's still possible.) Jenner's passion for research was roused. From the milkmaid's account, he deduced that a body infected by cowpox must form defenses against any form of pox, and so he conducted a risky experiment. In 1796, he scratched open the blisters of another milkmaid who had caught cowpox. Her name was Sarah Nelmes. Jenner extracted some

The Latin for "cow" is *vacca*, and that was Jenner's reason for calling his invention "vaccination."

82

More and more people were immunized against smallpox, and yet the disease persisted until well into the twentieth century. In 1967, the World Health Organization decided to eradicate the disease. In Europe, immunization was already compulsory. Doctors traveled to India and Africa to immunize people in those areas where the disease was still rife.

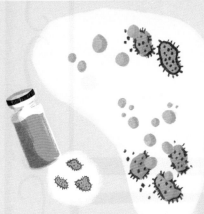

Today there are vaccines against many diseases, including mumps, measles, and German measles which used to be very dangerous for humans.

pus and applied it to the upper arms of eight-year-old James Phipps, his gardener's son. Phipps became feverish and felt ill, but he quickly recovered. What Jenner then tried was very dangerous and would not be allowed today, but he was certain that it would not harm the boy. He repeated the process on Phipps, but this time with pus from smallpox—the deadly disease. He did not fall ill: he was immune. It was like a miracle! Jenner also successfully carried out his test on other children and adults. At first the Royal Society—the foremost scientific institution in Great Britain—was not convinced by Jenner's research and wanted evidence, so Jenner decided to publish his results himself. These were picked up all over the world. At last Jenner was made a member of the Royal Society, and the process that he called "vaccination" became the recognized method of protecting people against smallpox.

Edward Jenner

James Phipps

TRANSISTOR

Transistors are the most important components on a microchip. They can switch and strengthen signals and regulate the flow of electricity.

The transistor was invented by John Bardeen and Walter Brattain. Bardeen was an American physicist and an outstanding scientist who was twice awarded the Nobel Prize in Physics. Even in his youth he was so gifted that he had to be put in classes several years ahead of his age group. He was only 15 when he went to the University of Wisconsin to study electrotechnology, math, and physics. A few years later, he continued his studies at the famous universities of Princeton and Harvard, and not long afterwards, he was working at another famous institution: Bell Labs in New Jersey, which were the source of many important inventions during the twentieth century, such as the first communications satellite, solar cells, and cellular communications technology. It was there that Bardeen and the

John Bardeen

Walter Brattain

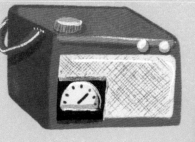

physicist Brattain together carried out research into the conductivity of certain solids (known as semiconductors) and metals. On Christmas Eve 1947, they presented the first bipolar transistor. They would have had no idea how many future Christmas presents would be based on their work. Suffice it to say that their invention sparked off an electronic revolution.

Transistors are used in computers, and also in radios, lighting and temperature sensors, chargers and indicators, and even in space travel.

Bipolar transistors consist of three parts: collector, base, and emitter.

The word "transistor" is a combination of two words— "transfer" and "resistor."

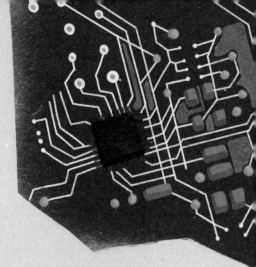

MICROCHIP

As we said before, "micro" comes from the Greek word for "small." A microchip is as thin as paper and smaller than a fingernail. But there is scarcely any invention that has changed human life as much as this tiny chip.

You will find it in any number of the things we use in our everyday lives: computers, smartphones, credit cards ... The American inventors Robert Noyce and Jack Kilby worked for different firms during the 1950s to develop what was known as the "integrated circuit" (IC), which was the basis for the making of microchips. But no one at the time had any idea how far-reaching this invention would be.

It is said that Kilby's first presentation of the IC was not particularly exciting. Even he probably had no real concept of what he might do with it. But perhaps he had a feeling that it had great potential!

What he showed was a piece of germanium (a semiconductor) that was less than half an inch (11 millimeters) long, fitted with a single transistor (which directs electrical tensions and currents) and other small parts. He turned on a switch and the first IC immediately began to draw a sine wave (a single curve repeated over and over again, just like an ordinary wave). And that was it. There were not yet any

If we now tried to dispense with microchips, our world would look very different. You can conduct an experiment with your family: try to spend just one day without using something that contains a microchip. If you've ever tried to do your own laundry by hand, you may have some idea of what a tough day would be in store for you.

A microchip can be injected under the skin of your pet—the details on it help identify them if they get lost.

Robert Noyce

Jack Kilby

products for which this invention could be used!

Nevertheless, Kilby went on experimenting with the IC, and eventually, Texas Instruments, the electronics manufacturer he worked for, built a piece of equipment that worked with ICs: a pocket calculator. Unlike the calculating machines that had previously been in use and that were about the same size as a typewriter (about half the size of Yoda in *Star Wars*), the pocket calculator was small and light.

It is said that Noyce and Kilby never quarreled over the invention of the IC. Their respective companies, Fairchild Semiconductor and Texas Instruments, however, were in constant dispute over whose laboratory had produced the first one. Kilby was later awarded the Nobel Prize in Physics, and Noyce founded the software firm Intel, one of the biggest producers of microchips in the world.

Now it was clear what could be achieved with ICs, because the technology showed that many functions could be collected in a very small instrument.

ICs played an important role in the development of computers. The first microchip, made in 1959, contained fewer than 4,000 tiny transistors on a silicon chip. As the technique has become more and more refined, several billion transistors can be placed on microchips just a few millimeters square.

LIGHT BULB

Thanks to the light bulb, the world suddenly became a lot brighter. This invention began the electrification of Planet Earth.

Sir Humphry Davy

Once the light bulb had been invented, people could have as much light in their homes as they wanted— and it was much brighter than any light they had before. The invention was not just a complicated affair but it also ended up being a competition. Just imagine you are trying to solve a difficult problem with rich rewards at the end, and you know that there are others trying to do the same. You'd certainly be in a hurry to get there first!

Warren De la Rue

In the first half of the nineteenth century, the British chemist Sir Humphry Davy used electricity, only recently discovered, to connect wires and a piece of carbon to a battery he had invented, making it shine.

In 1835, the Scotsman James Bowman Lindsay succeeded in getting an electric lamp to burn continuously for a few minutes.

In 1840, the British chemist and astronomer Warren De la Rue used Davy's discovery to obtain light from a platinum wire.

James Bowman Lindsay

In 1850, yet another British inventor, Joseph Wilson Swan, had the idea to place a carbonized paper filament inside a glass bulb. Within 10 years he had created a working bulb. This approach prevented the filament from breaking or burning too quickly. In 1878 he conducted a more successful experiment: he pumped air out of a glass bulb in which he had placed a carbonized cotton filament. When he passed electricity through it, the filament lit up.

The German clockmaker and inventor Heinrich Göbel, who had emigrated to the U.S. in 1848,

Heinrich Göbel

Nothing moves faster than light. The speed of light is 186,000 miles (300,000 kilometers) per second. That is the speed at which the starship Millennium Falcon flies in *Star Wars*, though, according to Han Solo, it can actually reach one and a half times that speed.

Joseph Wilson Swan

Thomas Alva Edison

wrote in his notes that at this time, he, too, had been experimenting with light bulbs that contained carbonized threads.

Later, in 1879, Thomas Alva Edison produced the first light bulb that was able to shine for long periods. He designed a process that created a vacuum inside the glass bulb so that the filament, made of carbonized bamboo threads, would burn longer. This bulb lasted for about 1,000 hours. Edison was already well known in the U.S. as an inventor. He had established a research laboratory and worked with a team of researchers. Together they had tested 6,000 materials and had finally decided that carbonized bamboo was the one that worked best.

Edison's company then began to mass-produce the lamps.

Of course, his light bulbs could only burn if there was electricity, and so in 1882 he also built an electric power station in New York City, where he lived.

Edison had acquired the patent for his light bulb in 1880, but Swan filed a complaint. He had already applied for a patent in England in 1878 for his own bulb that used carbonized filament. In the course of this dispute, Göbel stepped in to claim that he had invented the light bulb. He was unsuccessful, however, and as far as we know his claim had no basis. Swan and Edison eventually joined forces and, in 1883, founded the company Edison & Swan, which manufactured light bulbs in England. Edison is now better known than Swan because he was the one who greatly expanded the electricity industry. He was also extremely skilled when it came to

In large cities such as London, New York, and Shanghai, there is so much artificial light during the night that it is difficult to see the stars in the sky.

self-publicizing, and he went out of his way to ensure that he was a regular subject of newspaper articles and people's conversations.

Too much light can be unhealthy. For example, insects circle around streetlights until they're exhausted because they think the light is the Moon, which they use for orientation. People also need a break from light so that their bodies can rest and they can sleep peacefully. Especially confusing for the body is the light from cell phones and tablets. This light contains a large number of blue wavelengths, as does daylight. It can keep us awake even if we're tired, because it acts as a signal to the body: it's now daytime.

Nowadays, we often use energy-saving light bulbs. They use less electricity than the classic bulb, which in many countries has been banned.

Lights that work through semiconductor technology also use less energy than the classic bulb. These are called LED (light-emitting diode) lights and are very bright.

The amount of artificial light shining all over our planet is best seen from outer space. Satellite pictures tell the story.

Having light available all the time means that you can read, work, build, write, or draw whenever you want to.

ALTERNATING CURRENT

Nikola Tesla invented the technology for the production and development of alternating current, which is the electricity that comes out of our plugs.

Tesla registered more than a hundred patents during his lifetime. His head was simply bursting with ideas. For example, he wanted to use solar energy as a source of electricity, and to find wireless ways of distributing electrical power—issues that scientists are still working on today. He had a variety of jobs before finally devoting himself completely to his inventions: mechanical engineer, roadworker, supply teacher, telegraphy technician. He worked at Europe's first switchboard, where his boss was the well-known Hungarian inventor Tivadar Puskás. It was there that Tesla began to think about designing an alternating-current engine. He took this idea with him to New York City, where once again he found himself working for a famous inventor: Thomas Alva Edison (though only for a few months). In 1888 Tesla

Tesla became more and more famous because of his inventions. In time he earned a lot of money, and he liked to spend it—for example, he would wear a tie for just one week and then throw it away, and he lived in expensive hotels instead of an apartment or a house.

In his laboratory, Tesla had various coils and constructions, and in the middle he even had an iron mast that could extend to 164 feet (50 meters) in height. This was designed to catch lightning discharges.

Do you associate the name Tesla with automobiles? You're right. Tesla, Inc., an American manufacturer of electric automobiles with alternating-current engines, is named after him.

Nikola Tesla

Tesla maintained that he had made contact with extraterrestrial life. His fellow scientists regarded this as really weird, but Tesla insisted that he had received signals from Mars. A few decades later, scientists suspected that these might have been natural radio waves from Jupiter.

Tivadar Puskás

acquired the patent for his electric magnetic motor. He set up his own research laboratory and experimented with ways of sending electricity through the air and the earth. He invented what is known as the Tesla coil, which produces a high-frequency alternating current. His great goal—which sadly he never achieved—was to transmit news and energy without wires from the east coast of the U.S. to a receiving station in France in time for the Paris Exposition in 1900. He acquired his first patent for wireless energy transmission on March 20, 1900. Today this is recognized as the first patent for radio technology.

There are various explanations for why people greet each other over the phone or in person with the word "hello." One of these goes back to Tesla's old boss Puskás. In 1877, working in Boston, he was testing the prototype of a telephone, and when he first heard the voice of Edison at the other end of the line, he is said to have asked "Hallod?", which in Hungarian means "Can you hear me?" This was followed by "Hallom," which means "I can hear you." And that gave rise to "hello."

Tesla coils were to be seen in a very famous movie made in 1931: Frankenstein. They produced the scary flashes of lightning in Dr. Frankenstein's laboratory while he was creating his monster.

ELECTRIC GUITAR

"Louder, please!" This request was the spur
for the invention of the electric guitar.
With this, one can greatly increase the volume
and also produce new sounds.

About a hundred years ago, there were many
changes in the world of music. Big band jazz
was becoming more popular, and the sound
of this kind of music really was big. Together
with piano, percussion, and guitar, there were
several trumpets, trombones, and saxophones.
Unfortunately, however, against all of these
instruments you could hardly hear a note
from the acoustic guitars. Instead of saying
to himself, "In that case I'll only play in
small bands," the Texan musician George
Beauchamp decided to look for a way to
magnify the sound of his guitar. After
much twiddling around and a number
of failures, he finally invented the
electromagnetic sound reproducer.

George Beauchamp

Adolph Rickenbacker

Beauchamp took out
a patent on his sound
reproducer in 1934.

This is still in use today and works along similar principles to those of a dynamo on a bicycle. It has a spool of coiled copper wire that is wrapped around one or several magnets. (Beauchamp used two horseshoe magnets.) The metal strings of the guitar run in between. Just as with a dynamo—when the energy created by the rotation of the wheel lights the cycle lamp—the guitar uses movement for the same effect, although this may be less easily visible to the human eye. When the metal strings are plucked, there are vibrations. The magnets and the copper wire produce an electromagnetic field, and the vibrations are recognized by the sound reproducer or, to be more precise, it recognizes the number and speed of the vibrations and carries these to the amplifier (see next page). The finish comes when the amplifier turns the vibrations back into audible sounds.

Together with the guitar maker Paul Barth and the inventor Adolph Rickenbacker, Beauchamp developed the first electrically amplifiable Hawaiian guitar. Owing to its appearance, it was dubbed the Frying Pan.

In the early 1950s, the American instrument maker Leo Fender designed the electric guitar and electric bass that

Musicians loved the new invention. For instance ...

... The Beatles, ...

... the brilliant guitarist Sister Rosetta Tharpe, ...

... and Chuck Berry.

are named after him. Unlike the acoustic guitar, they have no resonant interior, which means they are not hollow but are mainly made out of solid wood or various synthetic materials. For that reason, they sound different and are practically indestructible. The musician and inventor Les Paul helped to develop this "solid body" form of the instrument, and since those days, all kinds of electric guitars have appeared on the scene. For example, there are some with two necks, some with seven strings (instead of six), and even some that can be folded up.

Jim Marshall

When Brian May, guitarist in the band Queen, was a teenager, he and his father constructed a highly original electric guitar: they used the blade of a bread knife, wood from an old fireplace, knitting needles, and the valve spring from a motorcycle.

Another important factor for the sound is the amplifier. This is also an electronic piece of equipment. When you hear a melody being played on an electric guitar, the sound is not formed by the instrument alone but also by the amplifier. Many guitarists regard it as part of the instrument rather than just a loudspeaker. How does it work? The signal from one or

St. Vincent is the first female musician to have designed a production model for a guitar. Many like using her guitar, including Jack White, who is one of the most popular guitarists in the world.

Jimi Hendrix (center) was one of the most famous guitarists in the world.

several sound reproducers is carried to the amplifier by a special cable or by radio. One of the most important contributors to this development was Jim Marshall. He owned a music business, had close contact with many musicians, and therefore had a very good idea of what they wanted. Because of all the amplifiers, loudspeaker boxes, and effects equipment he built, he was given the nickname "The Lord of Loud." Since the 1960s more and more devices have been used to produce different sounds and effects.

In 1976, The Who were reckoned to be the loudest band in the world, with a performance of theirs having reached 126 decibels. Just over 30 years later, the heavy metal band Manowar reached 139 decibels during the sound check for one of their concerts. Also AC/DC, with about 130 decibels, are louder than a police siren (116 decibels) and as loud as a fighter jet.

Most electric guitars have several sound reproducers and selector switches to change the volume and tone, which can vary from very loud to very quiet, and from smooth to harsh.